Blue Peter

D0507808

£5.99
UK only

Contents

**Written by Steve Hocking, Anne Dixon
and Bridget Caldwell**

Simon Thomas

Konnie Huq

Matt Baker

Left: Katy revisits a special place – Jerusalem's Wailing Wall.

Below: Top tips for Simon from Britain's Olympic Sprint Cycle Team.

Below: Always game to try out new ways of keeping fit – Simon, Katy and Matt have a good old bounce on the latest craze,

Lucy

Mabel

George

Kari

Oke

HELLO there!

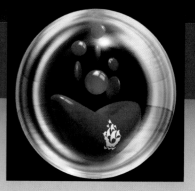

Welcome to the thirtieth Blue Peter book and the first of the new millennium. This has been a very special year for Blue Peter fans, young and old! We took older viewers on a trip down memory lane when the 'Box for the Year 2000' was finally opened; for younger viewers, it was the year we said goodbye to Katy, one of the best loved of all Blue Peter presenters. You can read about both of these events in this book and enjoy some of the many highlights of a great year.

Blue Peter is the most popular television programme made for children in the UK and this book takes you behind the scenes and out on location. You can visit Australia with the team, run the London Marathon with Simon and travel to Russia with Matt. Travel back in time with Konnie who finds out about life a century ago. There's marvellous news about our New Life Appeal and in true Blue Peter tradition we've included some foolproof recipes and make ideas. We hope that we've chosen some of your favourite moments and that you will spend many hours cooking, making and reading.

Above: A proud moment as Kevin Keegan, manager of England's football team, shows off his Blue Peter badge!

Above: He's behind you! Konnie dwarfed by a 7 metre-long triceratops.

Left: The Palace of Versailles is so beautiful it takes your breath away. Its last Royal owners, Louis XVI and Marie Antoinette, were forced to leave during the French Revolution and were beheaded in 1793.

Below: Didn't he do well! Matt joined a group of potential Royal Marines whose future careers and lives hung in the balance.

Diary from DOWN UNDER

The **1999 Summer Expedition** was to the world's smallest continent – Australia. It's big on things to see and do!

We started in **Darwin,** Australia's most northern city. Konnie and Matt headed straight for the beach, where once a day you can hand-feed fish with bread. Konnie discovered that the fish didn't like eating the crusts and they both got completely soaked when a wave crashed into them!

We were up at five the next morning to travel to **Kakadu,** Australia's largest National Park. Covering 4.3 million acres, it's about the same size as Wales and is a haven for wildlife. Around 275 different species of birds live here, along with 60 different mammals, 75 reptiles, 1,200 plants and at least 10,000 different types of insects! Konnie and Simon went in search of the world's largest living reptile – the Saltwater Crocodile, which will attack and eat most creatures – even Blue Peter presenters! They also had a lesson on how to find food in the bush – Simon pointed out you should only do this with an expert who knows what's safe to eat. They tried all sorts of things including water lilies and green ants, which are full of vitamin C. However, one ant wasn't too pleased and bit Konnie's tongue!

Matt had a lesson on how to play one of the world's oldest musical instruments, the didgeri-doo, from 8-year-old Rolland Ah Chee. It took a bit of time but after about 20 minutes he was getting a noise. And we were all impressed when

■ *Opposite page, top:* A map of our expedition down under.
Middle: Matt taking a breather at Surfers' Paradise.
Bottom: After a long day's work, time to relax in the pool.

■ The four of us outside Sydney Opera House – did you know it's covered with over a million tiles which wash themselves when it rains?

he threw a boomerang and it came back to him – what a natural!

We then travelled into the **Red Centre.** It's amazing – everywhere you go you see red – red sand, red soil and red rocks. This is where we came across some animals we hadn't expected to find in Australia – camels! The Outback is home to the only wild camels in the world. They were brought there in the 1870s to carry the heavy equipment needed to build the telegraph stations. These days they carry people taking in the sights of the Red Centre, much of which dates back about 800 million years. Konnie set off on a camel called Tommy, Simon's was called Cooper, and Matt rode Rocket. We had a great time – Konnie felt it was like being in a postcard. The only problem was that they kept drooling green saliva down our legs and making embarrassing noises!

After the camel ride we decided to go and watch the sunset at Uluru, otherwise known as **Ayers Rock**. It's the world's biggest monolith – 348 metres high. As we reversed, there was a nasty crunching noise. "Has anyone seen the tripod?" asked Will, the cameraman. You guessed it, we'd just run over the 'legs' for the camera. Oops! But despite a crushed tripod, the sunset was worth rushing for. It changed through an amazing selection of reds, oranges and purples. Everyone thought it was awesome. As Simon put it, "Ayers Rock rocks!"

■ *Top left:* The crew of the *Bounty* see what Matt's made of.
Top right: Camel trekking is certainly one of the more unusual ways of taking in the sights of the Outback. *Middle left:* Ready for action – Matt about to see if he can make his boomerang come back. *Bottom left:* As Katy found out, a great way to look at Sydney Harbour is by boat.

Then it was off to **Melbourne** where we met up with Katy. She'd flown over with the Manchester United football team who were playing against the Soccer-Roos at the Melbourne Cricket Ground (Man U won 2-0!). The MCG is one of Australia's most famous sports stadiums. As well as cricket, it's also the home of Aussie Rules Football, which is a bit like Gaelic football. Simon went training with the Essendon team and joined in a game with a local school team in which he scored a goal. After the match he showed us his feet, which were covered with blisters from all the kicking he'd done!

Katy visited one of the most famous roads in Australia – Ramsay Street. She had a good nose around the television studios where most of the series is filmed and even got to walk over the famous bridge and sit in the coffee shop, talking to Ian Smith who plays Harold.

Konnie went to **Healesville Wildlife Sanctuary** and met some of Australia's native animals. She helped feed the wallabies and baby dingoes that tried to chew her Blue Peter badge!

The weirdest looking animal she came across was the duck-billed platypus which she loved – she thought it looked like a cross between a beaver, a duck and a soft toy! While we there it was Konnie's birthday and in the evening we went out to a restaurant to

■ Simon *(top)* kitted out for his first game of Aussie Rules Football, while Katy *(above)* drops in to say G'day to Harold (Ian Smith) on the set of 'Neighbours'. *Left:* the crew enjoying the sunset at Ayers Rock.

■ Top: Konnie feeding the wallabies at Healsville Wildlife Sanctuary. *Above:* **Happy Birthday to you! – Konnie's surprise birthday cake.** *Right:* **Pelicans are just one of the many types of wildlife you can see at Moreton Island.** *Below:* **Simon and Konnie at Sydney Opera House.**

celebrate. Will had arranged a surprise cake and the whole restaurant sang 'Happy Birthday' to her four times!

Next stop **Sydney,** where Katy and Simon got to climb the largest steel-arch bridge in the world, Sydney Harbour Bridge. Safety is of the utmost importance – you're not allowed to take anything up which could fall on the cars below, even your own handkerchief! But they did make an exception and let us take up our camera – once it had been attached to a very strong safety line. It was a great feeling getting to the top and at over 130 metres above sea level you get some fantastic views of the harbour.

We also filmed at the Sydney Opera House. Designed by the Danish architect, Joern Utzon, it's a strange-looking building. Apparently he came up with the roof design while he was peeling an orange. We tried to re-create it with orange segments but the wind kept blowing them over! That night we had a farewell dinner for Konnie and Simon. They'd finished filming and were going home while the rest of us were heading off to Surfers' Paradise on Australia's Gold Coast.

So far, we'd been extremely lucky with the weather but that was all to change and the rain started coming down. This didn't stop Matt training with surf life-savers or Katy having a lesson on how to sand-ski, which involved holding on to a giant kite and being pulled along the beach. And there was loads to do at **Tangalooma** on Moreton Island, including feeding the pelicans, sand-tobogganing down some of the world's biggest sand dunes, snorkelling round the wrecks and meeting Tangalooma's wild dolphins, who turn up every night to be hand-fed their favourite fish.

The final place we visited on the expedition was **Cairns,** which is where Katy and Matt went on the Flying Leap. They were strapped on to a sort of hang-glider with Will, who was going to film them. All three were then pushed off a ledge and travelled at breakneck speed for 60 metres over the rainforest ... screaming! They loved it.

On the last day we went out to the **Great Barrier Reef** where Katy did some deep-sea exploring with Robin Aiello, a marine biologist. Matt had never dived before so he was given a lesson and was taken down by an instructor on an introductory dive. He loved it. **The perfect end to a fantastic expedition!**

Above: right: Katy, Matt and Will, the cameraman, get ready to take a flying leap. *Left:* Success! Simon and Katy reach the top of the Sydney Harbour Bridge. The view was spectacular and well worth the climb.

TIME CAPSULE

Way back in 1971, the Blue Peter team buried a lead-lined box filled with souvenirs of the programme, which was not to be opened until the year 2000. It was moved to a second secret location in 1984 when another box of Blue Peter mementoes was buried with it.

There wasn't a chance Blue Peter would forget about digging it up – our office was swamped with letters from Blue Peter viewers, young and old, reminding us.

So, early on a cold morning at the start of the new millennium we were all out in the Blue Peter garden armed with spades and shovels. Excitement was in the air.

Following the map, we paced our way to the 'exact' location of the boxes and started digging. And digging and digging! 'Let's double-check with the map', said Matt. Another hole was dug close by. It was hard-going and reinforcements had to be brought in.

Clare Bradley arrived to check we weren't doing too much damage to the garden. A company with special searching

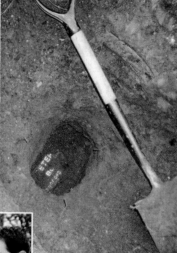

equipment tried to locate our buried boxes. Mabel and Lucy tried to sniff them out for us. Konnie kept shouting, 'I've found it', only to reveal stones and bricks. We started digging another hole and, just as we were about to give up for the day, Katy struck treasure. There at the bottom of an almost 2 metre-deep hole was one of our boxes. We could just make out the words 'not to be opened until 2000'.

We hadn't been digging deeply enough. We were overjoyed and so were countless people at Television Centre who had been keeping an eye on the proceedings, hoping for a glance at the box they'd seen buried when they were children.

The presenters from 1971 – Valerie Singleton, John Noakes and Peter Purves – joined us for a ceremonial box opening.

Sadly, the contents were rather damp but memories came flooding back. Simon Groom and Janet Ellis, who had buried the 1984 box, revealed the soggy contents. It was quite an emotional occasion and the contents were soon being dried and preserved by experts before touring the country with the BBC's Future World exhibition.

Don't worry, we didn't leave a huge hole in the garden! We did what any Blue Peter team would do – buried another time capsule, not to be opened until 2029. What age will you be then?

15

We celebrated St Patrick's Day in style this year when Shane, Mark, Kian, Nicky and Bryan, otherwise known as 'Westlife,' popped into the studio to perform their record-breaking single, 'Fool Again'. In between rehearsals, Konnie had time to have a quick chat with them.

Are you surprised at how big you've become?

KIAN: It's been amazing to see how far we've come in such a relatively short time – it blows us away really.

Do you think success has changed you in any way?

NICKY: No, not really. My two best mates still treat me as they've always done. They don't really care about what I do.

MARK: We keep our feet on the ground. But obviously it has changed us in the way we are recognised so we wear baseball hats more often!

Do you enjoy travelling round the world?

BRYAN: Yes we've been to places we never knew existed and flying is the only chance we have to get some decent sleep! The downside is having to live out of a suitcase.

MARK: Planes are like beds to us now – I even managed to sleep for 13 hours once on a flight!

Do any of you have any bad habits?
SHANE: We're all pretty bad at falling back asleep after our tour manager has told us we have to get up and work.

What are your hopes for the future?
NICKY: That's easy – to be the biggest band in the world!

Who are your musical heroes?
BRYAN: We all have different ones, from Michael Jackson to Billy Joel to Mariah Carey.
SHANE: I think the Backstreet Boys are the best boyband around at the moment. They have a brilliant live show.

Our St Patrick's Day guests were absolutely gorgeous and we couldn't miss the chance of a quick photo together.

What do you do in your spare time?
KIAN: We don't have any but we try to get home and see our families whenever we can.

What's your favourite single?
NICKY: It has to be 'Flying Without Wings' as it won us Record of the Year and it was such an emotional and wonderful feeling winning that in our first year.

What's the best thing about coming on Blue Peter?
SHANE: It has to be getting a Blue Peter badge – I've always wanted one!

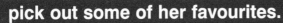

I've tackled many sports during my time on Blue Peter and snowboarding is definitely one of my favourites. This is when I took to the slopes in Whistler during the summer expedition to Canada.

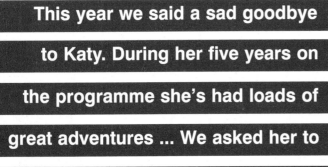

KATY'S

I've spent a lot of time up in the air. In 1998 I travelled to Cyprus to join the Red Arrows and was lucky enough to take the hot seat in the Team Leader's jet as they practised their famous formation flying.

Clear for take off! This is me ready to hit the skies in a Harrier.

This was one of my proudest moments on Blue Peter. I'd just been told that my horseriding skills were good enough for me to join the inspection party for the Household Cavalry's annual inspection parade. It was a great honour and I can't tell you how nervous I felt!

Touring cars, monster trucks and even JCBs – you name it, I've probably driven it! Here I am posing by a Beetle which I got to test-drive in Mexico.

SCRAPBOOK

I've really enjoyed all the different countries I've visited during my time on Blue Peter. This is me in Hollywood when I went behind the scenes on the movies 'James and the Giant Peach' and 'Matilda'. What do I look like!

These photos are from two of my diving experiences. The one on the left is when I was challenged by Blue Peter viewer, Vicky Baker, to go diving the old-fashioned way and the other is me taking a well-earned break from cleaning out the shark tank in the London Aquarium.

This is me and Glamour Girl, the horse I learned to train with the help of horse whisperer, Monty Roberts. He showed me how he can gently break in a wild horse in just 25 minutes, something that normally takes weeks.

I've been lucky enough to interview all sorts of famous people, including Danny de Vito, Britney Spears and Damon Hill. Damon came into the studio shortly after he'd won the Formula One World Championship. The reason he's looking so pleased is that we've just awarded him a gold Blue Peter badge for this great achievement.

Cardigan Cushions

As any fan of 'Changing Rooms' will know, it's the accessories that make a room. And what about these funky cushions that could transform a boring bedroom into a cosy den? They cost a fortune to buy, but here's how to convert an old cardigan or jumper into a cushion that would turn Laurence Llewelyn-Bowen green with envy.

● **Lay an old cardigan out flat,** making sure the bottom edges are even. Do up the buttons. Use a ruler and a piece of chalk to draw a line from under one arm right across to the other. Carefully cut along this chalk line

● **You will be left with a kind of tube.** The cut edge will be the top of the cushion and that's why you have to make sure the bottom edges are absolutely even or your cushion will be wonky. If you can unravel part of the top half of the cardigan, you can use this wool for sewing.

● **Turn the tube shape inside out** so that the buttons are on the inside and pin together the edges you have just cut. Thread a bodkin or a big-eyed needle with some wool and sew these edges together to stop it unravelling. Small running stitches are best and two rows will make it really strong. Overstitch the bottom edge.

● **Undo one or two of the buttons** and turn the cushion right side out. You will already have the basic cushion shape and it's ready to be filled. You could use a stuffed pad from an old cushion or odds and ends, like the top half of your cardigan.

● **If you are using an old jumper the method is almost the same.** Simply cut off the top from underarm to underarm, turn inside out and sew the cut edges.

● **Turn it back to the right side out** but instead of sewing the bottom end of the jumper, cut or undo the stitching on both sides as far as the end of the ribbing. If necessary over-stitch these edges to prevent unravelling. On one side of your cushion shape, sew 5 or 6 buttons above the ribbing, spacing them equally. On the other bottom edge make some loops with matching or contrasting coloured wool. Space them to correspond with the buttons. Fill your cushion and tuck the button side under the pad and do up the buttons.

● **Tassels on the corners give the cushions a professional look** and they are easier than you'd think to make. All you need is a piece of cardboard and a long length of wool. The cardboard should be as wide as you want the tassel to be long. Simply wind the wool around the card roughly 15 times – the more wool, the thicker the tassel. Make a note of how many winds you do and wind the same amount for each tassel. Leave a long end before cutting the wool. Thread this end on to a needle and wrap it a couple of times around the wool in the middle of the card. Tie it firmly. Now slip the card out of the loop of wool. Hold the loop by the knot and cut through the end opposite the knot. To finish off the tassel, fold the two bunches of wool together and wind another piece of wool around it roughly 1 cm below the knot and fasten securely.

● Then put the threaded needle through the knot at the top and sew the tassel to the corner of the cushion.

TO RUSSIA

This is me in St Petersburg's main palace square.

The city is full of fabul... buildings including the stunn... Winter Palace, the treas... house of the Russian Tsa...

When I was told I was going filming in the 'Venice of the North', little did I think that I would find myself in St Petersburg in Russia. It got its nickname from the fact that it's built on water and one of the best ways of seeing the sights is by taking a boat trip along the city's canals.

I'd been invited to attend the launch of a special ship called the *Shtandart*, a replica of the royal yacht belonging to the 18th-century Russian Tsar, Peter the Great. It was being rebuilt by a team of volunteers, including 14-year-old Sasha Korshunov, who I went to visit. My Russian isn't very good, but fortunately Sasha spoke English. She told me that her family lives in a communal flat, sharing the rooms with another family. There's not much space and they all use the same kitchen, bathroom and toilet.

St Petersburg used to be a flat, boggy marshland so no one could quite believe it when Peter the Great stuck his boot into the ground and declared "This will be St Petersburg." He forced prisoners and peasants from all over Russia to build his dream city. They had very few tools and had to gather dirt in their shirts and carry huge loads of stone by hand. Thousands died building Peter's 'paradise' and it's still referred to as 'the city built on bones'.

I was amazed when I visited the building where Peter liked to live. It was not a grand palace but a simple log cabin! He even made some of the furniture himself. Peter loved practical jokes – at dinner parties he'd hide rats and mice in the food and make sure there weren't enough chairs for the guests. He thought it was a great

Inside Peterhof, the grand palace that Peter built for his wife, Catherine.

The only way to travel! Me in a troika about to set off for the ballet ...

It's been some time since my last ballet lesson and I was finding it tough!

Dinnertime with 14-year-old Korshunov and her family.

laugh watching them fight for a place at his table!

As you'll probably know, I'm a bit of a dancer. However, it was quite a few years since I'd done ballet so I didn't know how I'd get on at the Vaganova school, one of the world's best ballet schools. You have to be extremely fit and talented to do well in ballet and I had to concentrate very hard to keep up with other pupils. The school demands incredibly high standards and I was very impressed by their discipline and dedication.

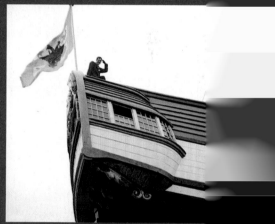

When it was time to launch the *Shtandart* everything went smoothly and according to plan.

This summer she set sail on an epic journey travelling from St Petersburg to Deptford in East London, close to where Peter the Great stayed when he visited Britain 300 years ago. Hopefully, she will now become a sail-training ship for young people from around the world – I wonder what Peter would have made of that!

Top left: Outside the shop of the world's most famous jeweller, Peter Carl Fabergé.
Middle left: One of the best ways of seeing the sights is by boat.
Middle and bottom right: It took the team of volunteers 5 years to reconstruct the royal yacht, the *Shtandart*, using shipbuilding techniques similar to those used in the 18th century.
Right: Taking a closer look at Peter the Great's actual throne.

Many servants spent their whole lives living and working at one house

First thing in the morning work begins cleaning the house

Just time to iron the newspaper before breakfast

A hundred years ago, Christmas was celebrated with all the joy that we share today, nowhere more so than in the great stately homes of Britain. Presents and games were all part of the fun but a lot of hard work made the festivities possible as Konnie, Simon and Matt found when they set about re-creating "A Country House Christmas" at Longleat House for a special programme.

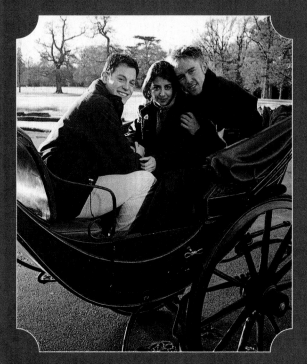

Arriving in style for our 'Country House Christmas'

Are you being served?

Life in a country house was very different for those who lived 'above' and 'below' stairs. 'Below stairs', largely out of sight of the owners of the houses and their guests, worked the servants. Forty-three servants worked inside Longleat House, many of them having lived and worked there since childhood. As Konnie found out, their days began and ended by candlelight and their rooms were usually in the attic, the coldest part of the house. Servants didn't have time to admire their luxurious surroundings. They had to work hard. With no washing machines or vacuum cleaners, everything was done by hand. Coal fires had to be made and carpets swept. Some servants' duties would seem very strange to us. Every day, the newspaper was delivered and then ironed! The ironing stopped the ink from the pages getting on to the hands of his lordship or her ladyship.

The 114 rooms at Longleat had to be inspected and kept spotlessly clean. With so many rooms and literally miles of

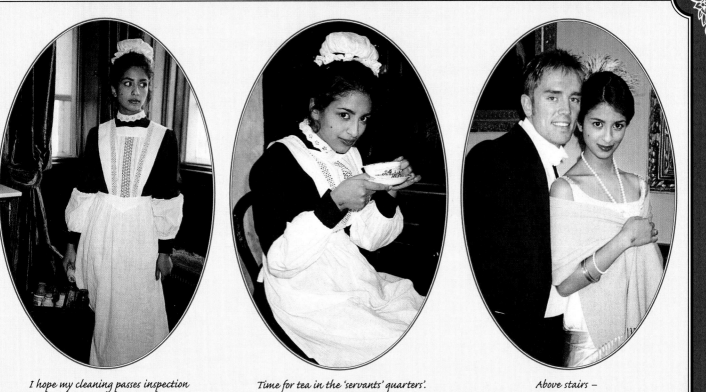

*I hope my cleaning passes inspection
by the housekeeper*

*Time for tea in the 'servants' quarters'.
I hope the bell doesn't ring*

*Above stairs –
the party begins*

stairs and corridors, servants had to be very fit. They could only relax in the servants' quarters, and even here a system of bells could be rung to call them to any part of the house. Konnie says "It was a hard life. Many servants were given just half a day off each week."

'Above stairs', lavish presents, cards and beautiful meals were all part of the Victorian Christmas. With no television or radio it was up to the party guests to entertain each other, with card games, magic tricks, songs and stories around the fire. "I had great fun telling a ghost story", says

Matt. "I think I managed to get the others quite scared. I really enjoyed the singing and eating the delicious chocolate log that Simon and Konnie had made in the kitchen!"

The programme ended with everyone singing 'We Wish You a Merry Christmas' around a massive tree in the Great Hall. "That really put us in the mood for Christmas", says Matt, "Mind you, looking at the work that went into decorating the house I know which side of the stairs I'd have wanted to live!"

We wish you a Merry Christmas!

OUR CANINES GO TO CRUFTS

2000 Crufts TV FILM CREW 2000

As Mabel and Lucy are both proud holders of the Kennel Club Good Citizen awards, we couldn't really turn down an invitation to visit Crufts 2000.

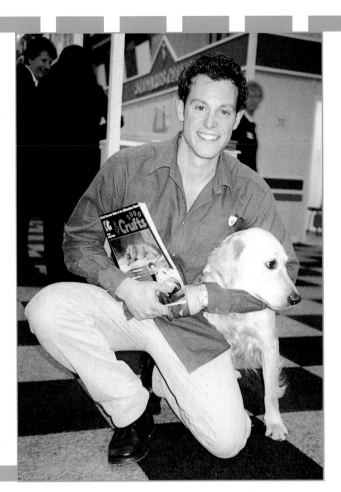

Crufts is the world's largest and longest-running dog show. This year, an estimated 25,000 dogs were taking part in a host of displays and competitions for pedigree, crossbreeds and mongrels.

After collecting a special TV Crew Crufts pass, Matt was delighted when he met up with ex-Blue Peter presenter and one of the BBC's top Crufts commentators, Peter Purves. Pete explained he had probably got his job way back in 1976 because of all the commentaries he had done on Blue Peter when canine champs had come to the studio.

Pete invited Matt into his commentary box where they had a brilliant

'Bend me, shape me, any way you want me!' The Essex Dogs Display Team took Matt

bird's-eye view of the display ring as well as a bank of TV monitors showing all the cameras' different pictures. Keeping an eye on the action meant the commentators would miss nothing even if the cameras did!

After a few words of wisdom from Pete, Matt donned a pair of headphones, picked up his lip microphone and was 'on air' commentating on an exciting agility display. He enjoyed himself so much Pete had trouble getting the mike back from him!

Lucy was on her best behaviour when she was in the ring with Matt. Under his expert guidance, she did a perfect parade of honour to the great delight of Blue Peter fans.

Matt was enjoying himself as much as the dogs and when the Essex Dogs Display Team asked if he'd help them out, he was delighted. All the dogs in this display team have been abandoned and after their training it's hoped they'll find new and loving homes. To show how well-behaved they are the Team puts humans into the ring. And, of course, Matt was first in line to lie down for a beautiful German shepherd dog to jump over!

Matt had a whale of a time and was keen to share his experiences with Katy and Joe Inglis, Blue Peter's vet. They met wonderful dogs like Endal, the Dog of the Millennium, who helps his disabled owner in so many ways. Katy and Joe fell in love with Tolstoy, Pet Survivor of the Year, who had suffered terribly in a house fire. Don't worry, Tolstoy has now made a full recovery! Having a dog is a big responsibility. The message Joe always gives to anyone who falls in love with one is to have a really good think about how much it will cost to feed and how much exercise it will need, to say nothing of all the grooming and cuddling. A dog is for life and will be a devoted friend if you can give it the love and respect it deserves.

Meeting lots of Blue Peter fans at Crufts was really good experience for Lucy (*above*) and it was thirsty work, too! (*below*)

at his word and thought he was the best human obstacle recruit they'd come across.

Bring and Buy for New Life

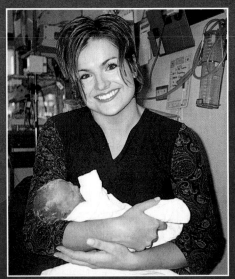

A big thank you to all of you who took part in our 'New Life' Appeal. Almost 50,000 of you wrote for 'Bring and Buy' sale packs and these are just a few of the photos that we received. We hope that you had as much fun at your sales as we all had at ours.

Left: It was wonderful to meet so many newborn babies in hospitals up and down the country.

Below left: Over fifty thousand of you organised bring and buy sales like the one we held in the Blue Peter studio.

£400,000
£300,000
£250,000
£200,000
£150,000
£100,000
£50,000
£25,000
£15,000
£10,000

Above: You got us to the top of the totaliser not once, but twice! We had to change all of the numbers on it!

Blue Peter

BLUE PETER
BRING & BUY FOR NEW LIFE

Our Appeal was for extra equipment for neonatal units in hospitals across the UK. We worked with the charity BLISS as we had in 1989. Some of you had written to tell us that you had been placed in a Blue Peter incubator when you were born and wanted to help the generation of children who would grow up in the new millennium. We thought that this was a great idea!

Our initial target was £500,000 – a huge amount of money which would help 40 hospitals. We launched the Appeal with a huge Bring and Buy sale in the Blue Peter studio and soon thousands of you had followed suit. We were certain that you could get us to the top of the totaliser, but we were amazed that you did so so quickly! The target of half a million pounds was reached by the start of the year, so we set a new target of one million pounds. In addition to helping neonatal units, we asked you to pay for 4 ambulances which would allow hospitals to set up the UK's first specialist neonatal training units.

You held a total of 47,857 Bring and Buy sales and at the beginning of June the fantastic sum of £2,317,288 had been raised, and hospitals had begun to receive much needed equipment. At least 114 hospitals across the UK will be provided with equipment which will help babies born at the start of a new century to have the best start in life. *Thanks again.*

With the extra money that you raised we plan to buy and equip four special ambulances to care for newborn babies.

APPEAL

Over
£2.3 million
raised!

You will need at least one pot, some thick string, metal washers (which you can buy from DIY stores), a short stick and, for optional extra decoration, raffia, pine cones and paint.

To make a garden chime with three different-sized pots, start with the middle-sized pot and cut off 50 cm of thick string. Split one end into strands.

The bell's clapper is a metal washer tied on to one strand of the string. Tie it around two or three times before knotting firmly. Do exactly the same with a second washer. The leftover string is now wrapped around the unsplit string about 2 or 3 cm above the washers. Tie it several times to make a large knot.

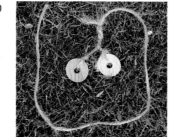

Now you're ready to attach the clappers to the pot. Thread the un-knotted end of string up through the inside of the pot and through the hole. The large knot should stop the string being pulled through the hole. If your knot isn't big enough, take the string out and tie it a few more times.

You could stop there but if you want to make a threesome, carry on making another two 'bells' in exactly the same way, cutting a long piece of string for the big bell and a shorter piece for the tiny one. If you have any spare washers you could tie these inside the big bell for extra ding!

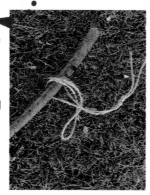

To hang the pots find a short piece of stick – a piece of wood pruned off a tree or a bush is ideal, but a bamboo cane or even a pencil will work well. Before attaching the bells, make a hanging loop for the stick. Cut a length of string and knot the ends together. Lay the string flat so the knot is at one end and a loop at the other. Place the stick across the middle and then thread the loop up through the knotted end. Pull the loop tight and the stick will be held firmly in place.

Attach the smallest bell first, close to the hanging loop. Tie two pots on one side of the hanging string and the biggest pot on the other to balance the garden chime. Allow enough length of string (space) between each pot so they don't hit each other. Make sure the pots are tied firmly and you're happy with the look and balance before cutting off any spare string. A dab of glue on the knots is a useful trick to stop the knots loosening. You could also put a little glue on the stick beneath the hanging loop to keep that in place.

If you can find some raffia and a couple of pine cones they will make your garden chimes look more professional. Slip a length of raffia around the base of a pine cone (under the scales) and tie it tightly. Attach two more cones to raffia and then tie all three together in a bunch. Hang the strings over the stick. Cut a bundle of short strands of raffia and tie in the middle. Glue the middle of the bundle over the string ends and knot on the stick. This will hold the pine cones in place.

DING-DONG!

DING-DONG!

DING-DONG!

There are so many variations you could make according to the size and number of pots you have. You could decorate the sides of the pot using one or two shells or paint a pattern (emulsion works well). I'm sure you'll have loads of ideas to make your garden chimes unique, as well as useful ways of putting them to good use – "Kari, Oke – ding-dong – teatime!"

Garden Chimes

If you'd like something pretty and practical for your garden or balcony, look no further – these garden chimes will fit the bill. You can make them using one terracotta plant pot or three or five if you want to go crazy. They are easy to make and look great wherever you hang them. They won't drive your neighbours bonkers as they only chime in very strong winds or if you give them a gentle pat.

31

Journey to the Roof

Half the challengers were from Britain and others had travelled from Kenya, Tanzania and Uganda. Simon was climbing with one of the partially sighted climbers, Charles Ronayne. "My task on the expedition was to be one of Charles' buddies, or guides, when the going got rough."

Just getting to the mountain was hard work. "It was a marathon journey. We bumped along some of the dustiest roads I've ever seen for over 8 hours", says Simon, "we camped at Loitokitok, 1800 metres above sea level, and we stayed there for two days to get used to the altitude and prepare for the climb."

The climb would take five days, and everyone was very tense. It was going to be hard work and everyone in the party would have to cope with 'altitude sickness' as their bodies adapted to there being less oxygen in the air at the top of the mountain.

"We set off in small groups with our back-up team following carrying the food and tents. It took us the best part of the day to reach our first campsite just above the tree-line. It was cold as well as wet but the next morning we got our first sight of the mountain's two peaks.

Kibo, the highest point in Africa, lay straight ahead as the challengers ate their evening meal. "Trouble was, however hard we tried, the evening meal of meat and two veg always tasted the same. And always very chewy! We all privately worried about the headaches and nausea that meant altitude sickness." Anyone suffering from severe altitude sickness would have to drop out.

The climb lasted four cold, wet, days. Several climbers had to drop out before they reached Kibo Hut. From there, the other climbers would make their bid for the roof of Africa.

"That night the temperature plummeted to well below freezing" remembers Simon.

It was a slow climb, which started before dawn.

Not everyone made it, but Simon and the others who did remembered it as one of the greatest achievements of their lives.

# of Africa

To celebrate the 50th birthday of the charity Sight Savers International, Simon was challenged to join a group of sighted and partially sighted 14–16 year olds, to climb Mount Kilimanjaro in Tanzania – the highest mountain in Africa. It was a tough mission.

Opposite page, bottom: Suzanne Long and Louise Waddington pass an unusual landmark. *Opposite page, top right:* Setting off from base camp at Loitokitok with the long climb ahead of us. *Opposite page, bottom right:* We stopped off to chat to local children. I think they enjoyed my trick! *Top left:* As we got closer to the summit we were full of confidence and high spirits. *Left:* We've done it! Freshly showered, we gathered for the presentation – what a sense of achievement we all felt. *Above:* The sun came out as the three UK challengers reached the top and displayed the flag of victory. *Top:* Me and the rest of the British challengers line up for a photo at Gatwick Airport before jetting off to Kenya.

THE STORY OF
Greyfriars Bobby

An incredible story about an extraordinary dog

It had all the hallmarks of a historical tale that we could tell on the programme. Matt could play Jock, Simon would make a perfect Mr Traill, but who could play Bobby?

Step forward Mabel the wonderdog. Now we know she's a girl but we felt she should be given the chance to dress up like the rest of us presenters, to bring history to life.

CAST:
Bobby the dog
Old Jock the shepherd
Mr Traill, Greyfriars
Dining Rooms owner

LOCATION:
Scotland

PERIOD:
end of the 19th century

Costume and make up took ages for Matt and Simon but for Mabel it was a quick collar change – tartan for turquoise!

Mabel was about to make her acting debut. The cameras rolled. "Action," shouted the director.

Bobby was a working dog who lived on a farm just outside Edinburgh. He lived with a shepherd called Old Jock. Every Wednesday Old Jock and Bobby travelled to Edinburgh for the weekly sheep market.

When the day's business was done, Old Jock would make his way to the Greyfriars Dining Rooms where he would buy his lunch. The owner knew Old Jock and his faithful dog well and always gave Bobby a tasty bowl of food – which he obviously enjoyed!

But Jock was old and couldn't carry on with his work on the farm. His boss ordered him to retire to Edinburgh. The farmer knew that Bobby was young and useful on the farm. He wanted to keep the dog, which would leave Old Jock all alone.

Bobby had other ideas. He wasn't working on the farm without Old Jock and soon gave the farmer the slip and began the very long journey to find his old friend. He eventually found Old Jock – cold and ill and sleeping rough.

Old Jock could hardly believe his eyes when he saw that faithful Bobby had found him and together they made their way to the only friend they knew – Mr Traill at the Greyfriars Dining Rooms. Mr Traill was shocked to see how sick the old man had become and went to fetch a doctor. On his return, Jock and Bobby had vanished. The old shepherd had been too frightened to stay.

A few days later Jock was found holding his bible in an old attic room. He had died, but not alone, as his best friend Bobby was there by his side.

Jock was buried in Greyfriars churchyard but Bobby refused to leave the grave. Mr Traill brought him food and tried to tempt the dog back to the farm. But Bobby kept returning to the churchyard.

John Gray
AT REST
1858

Here Lies
John Gray
AT REST
1858

For nine years Bobby stayed by his master's grave. Then council officials started to ask questions. Who owned Bobby? Was he licensed? Strays dogs were not wanted and an order was given for Bobby to be taken away and put to sleep.

Bobby was safe and became known as one of the famous sights of Edinburgh. He was even given the freedom of the city.
After another five faithful years of guarding Old Jock's grave, Bobby sadly died.

There was an outcry from local people who had come to know and love seeing Bobby permanently on guard at Old Jock's grave. Soon Edinburgh's Lord Provost heard Bobby's story and announced he would pay for a dog licence himself.

A statue was put up in the city of Edinburgh so nobody will ever forget the story of brave little Greyfriars Bobby.

Not only was the story a good one – but it's true. And who even managed to close her eyes as she portrayed Bobby's last moment? Our Mabel, of course. We should put her on the stage more often – she could win an Oscar!

TRUCK RACING

At the first mention of the word 'racing', Katy (no relation to Damon Hill!) was on her way to get the lowdown on a sport that began in the United States 20 years ago – truck racing. It was a sport that soon caught on in Europe and, in the early days, normal road trucks were raced. Today, truck racing is much more sophisticated and every year millions of pounds are spent trying to produce the winning truck.

The only British team constructors in this year's European Championship were about to reveal their new truck and test-drive it for the first time at Pembrey in West Wales. The pre-season testing is called the 'shakedown' and it's a nerve-racking time, as Harri Luostarinen (pictured right), the team's driver, told Katy.

The truck had taken six months to construct. A large support team with a complete workshop was on hand to monitor everything from its engine performance to the G-force it produced on corners.

Katy and the Blue Peter film crew were the first people outside the team to see the truck, but there was more excitement to come. Katy slipped on her overalls, adjusted her helmet like a pro and climbed into the passenger seat.

Harri sped around the mile-and-a-half circuit – it handled brilliantly. But there's more to racing than simply finishing first. Much of the technology that goes into building the fastest truck is used in the design and manufacture of new ones. Developments from racing have led to the introduction of lower exhaust emissions and better brakes.

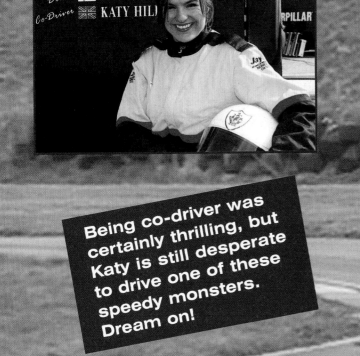

Being co-driver was certainly thrilling, but Katy is still desperate to drive one of these speedy monsters. Dream on!

37

ISLE OF MAN

'Traa dy liooar' which means 'time enough'. On the Isle of Man this is not so much a phrase – more a way of life.

The Isle of Man lies slap bang in the middle of the Irish Sea. It's home to over 74,000 people, many of whom speak the island's language – Manx Gaelic. The island has been a popular tourist destination since Victorian times and Konnie and Matt couldn't wait to explore.

Matt was surprised to find that kilts are traditional Manx dress and tried one for size. As it turned out, he rather fancied himself in it and wore it throughout his stay. His chosen tartan was in the Manx colours – blue for the sea, green for the hills, gold for the gorse, purple for the heather and white for the cottages.

Konnie and Matt soon discovered that the Isle of Man has all kinds of strange tales and superstitions. Many people believe in the fairy folk! So off they went to the Fairy Bridge, where legend has it that as you cross you must say

Getting ready to cast off and hoping the fish are biting!

In the Smoke House, I started to think about tomorrow's tasty breakfast.

'hello' to the little people. Although Matt and Konnie obliged, there was no reply.

Other famous island inhabitants are Manx cats. There are two kinds – 'Stumpies' with very tiny tails and 'Rumpies' with no tails at all. Tail or not, Konnie thought they were real cuties.

By far the most impressive sight on the island is the Laxey Wheel. Originally, the wheel pumped water from the lead mine that provided wealth and jobs for Manx people. Tales of days down the mine are an important part of the island's history, as Matt found out when he relived the hard life of a miner called Rob Kelly.

Give us a cuddle, Konnie – where else would you go to hug a Manx cat?

After a hard day's graft, a slap-up supper of delicious Manx kippers would be just the thing, and it still is today. Kippers are smoked herring, although Matt's meal didn't exactly come on a plate – he had to catch the fish and smoke them himself. Served and eaten with a generous dollop of lemon and lime marmalade, it rounded off a fascinating trip.

Saying 'hello' to the Little People.

A powerful reminder of days gone by.

Mabel
and
Lucy

SAUSAGE HOTPOT

Want to impress your family and friends with a scrumptious sausage supper that's really easy to cook and tastes terrific? It's a filling meal in itself and is easy on the washing up, too. Here's our foolproof recipe.

YOU WILL NEED

8 sausages (preferably the thick ones you buy in butchers' shops)

1 large onion

1 tablespoon plain flour

250 ml stock

squirt of tomato purée

2 tomatoes

4 medium-sized potatoes

a little oil and a knob of butter

Start by gently browning the sausages on both sides in an oiled pan. When they are ready, take them out of the pan and cut into bite-sized pieces. Put all the chunks into an ovenproof dish which has a lid. Next peel and slice the onion and gently brown it in the same pan you used for the sausages.

When the onions are soft add a tablespoon of plain flour and stir well. The idea is to make a thickish sauce to pour over the sausages. Dissolve a stock cube in 250 ml of hot water and add to the pan. Next put a good squirt of tomato purée, which will give the sauce a rich colour and help thicken things up. If you like tomatoes, slice a couple in half and add them. Hotpots are great for using up all sorts of things you might find lurking in the kitchen. Mushrooms, a stick of celery and carrot slices would all work well in this hotpot.

If you are using unseasoned sausages or vegetarian ones, add some black pepper to the sauce before carefully spooning it over the sausage chunks. You should have enough to cover the sausages, but not drown them.

Peel and thinly slice 4 medium-sized potatoes. Arrange them in overlapping layers on top of the sausages. Put a couple of dots of butter on the potatoes and cover with the lid. Put into a preheated oven at gas mark 3 or 170°C. Bake for 1 hour, then remove the lid and return to the oven for another 30 minutes, during which time the potatoes will turn brown and crispy.

Now line up the bowls and serve. You're bound to get requests for seconds!

Dear Blue Peter.

✏ We made a Santa's Grotto! It took us a while because we made extra things like a sleigh and Rudolph. We really enjoyed making it!

Caitlin (aged 10) and
Joanna Smith (aged 8)
Southport

✏ We have sent you a picture of the bats we made for Halloween after we saw you making them on the programme. We used some of dad's socks – good job they were clean!

Matthew (aged 9) and Steven Cook (aged 6)
Southampton

✏ Here's a picture of me with my space fishing game. I made it with some help from my dad, and when we played a game, I won!

Edward Love (aged 8)
Kesgrave, Suffolk

✏ I have been using the Blue Peter logo. I have drawn the logo in different ways – I've painted it on a wooden box with acrylic paints,

and on a sheet of glass and I have made a bead mat with it on. I liked seeing Konnie making a glass model of the logo.

Stuart Flegg (aged 7) Lytham St Annes

✏ My brother and I had great fun making the bird cakes. We made a total of eight and we gave some to our neighbours and family, leaving three for the birds in our garden. We hope the birds enjoyed eating them as much as we enjoyed making them! Thank you for showing the recipe on the show.

Claire (aged 12) and Ross Howard (aged 10)
Thornbury, Bristol

Here are just a few letters from the thousands of Blue Peter fans who write in to tell us what they've made and the fun they've had doing it!

Recently, my best friend Madeleine and I made two Blue Peter dogs, Bonnie and Lucy. We think they're so cute!

Alexandra Moore (aged 8)
Madeleine Browne (aged 8)
Reigate

I was inspired by Matt to make your sock ducks. Here is a picture of me with what I made – I am giving them as Easter presents.

Holly Dixon (aged 9)
Sheepy Magna, Warwickshire

We made the Blue Peter Santa Grotto during the Christmas holidays, we had a great time assembling it and we added some of our own touches. Thank you for a wonderful programme!

Andrew (aged 8) and Alex Snider (aged 6)
Waterloo, Belgium

I really like Blue Peter and I love making the things you do on the programme. On Bonfire Night, we had a party and I made chocolate brownies. I have also made my grandparents a Christmas card. Last week I made the bird cakes for the birds in our garden.

Richard Plews (aged 7) Wath-upon-Dearne, Rotherham

I am a teacher of Year 6 in Bournemouth. I thought your Mother's Day cards were really creative and I knew my children would love to make them – so here they are!

Miss P. Roberts Bournemouth

THIS IS ME AGED 8 MONTHS having a lovely time on holiday in Paignton, Devon

WE HAD LOTS OF PETS IN OUR FAMILY – hamsters, rabbits, guinea pigs, fish and dogs. This is me, my sisters Samantha and Debbie and my mum, with our new puppy Shogun, a Giant Schnauzer!

I USED TO LOVE DRESSING UP when I was younger. The reason I'm looking so pleased here is that I've just won first prize in my nursery school fancy-dress competition. What do you mean, you don't know what I am? I'm a chocolate soldier of course!

MY FIRST DRIVING LESSON! I was four years old when this was taken – what you can't see is that I was too small for my feet to reach the pedals!

MY SIXTH BIRTHDAY. I've always enjoyed making a noise and couldn't believe my luck when I was given my own drum kit!

ONE OF MY EARLIEST HOBBIES WAS GYMNASTICS. I started when I was 7. This is me, two years later, aged 9, when I'd just become North of England Gymnastic Champion in floor and vault. I was dead chuffed!

THIS WAS ONE OF MY BEST CHRISTMASES because I was given my first mountain bike. I loved it and spent the whole day riding around – my mum couldn't get me off it!

GYMNASTICS TOOK UP A LOT OF MY TIME – I used to spend 25 hours a week training with my mates. But it wasn't all work. We did get some time off like here when we'd gone on a barbecue together.

IN 1991 MY FAMILY MOVED TO A FARM IN DURHAM and I spent a lot of time helping my mum with all the jobs that had to be done.

Now that Matt has been on the programme for a year, we thought it was time to find out more about him. So we asked him to pick out some photos which showed the kind of things he used to get up to.

Matt's Family Album

ANOTHER HOBBY OF MINE WAS SHEEPDOG TRAINING. I've had 3 border collies – Meg, Lace and Fern, who I'm holding here. This photo was taken when she was only 8 weeks old. I worked hard with her to train her up and she still works on the farm today.

The MARATHON

Once Simon had decided to take part in the 20th London Marathon, the next question was 'what to wear?'

We knew that Blue Peter viewers would be keen to help so we launched the Marathon T-shirt design competition. Simon knew he would have a running number on his chest and thought budding designers would want to know what it was. The Marathon organisers very kindly issued 27-year-old Simon Thomas, the 27th Blue Peter presenter, a very special number – 2727.

Simon wanted a shirt that would help him stand out in a crowd of runners. Blue Peter viewers knew exactly the sort of thing he wanted and 43,856 viewers put pen to paper and sent in their eye-catching designs.

The Blue Peter office was swamped with mailbags and it took days and days to look at all the entries. We filled the studio with hundreds of runner-up designs but, after a great deal of cogitation and deliberation, Simon finally made his choice. It was a brilliant design featuring a Blue Peter ship speeding along on legs and was the work of 10-year-old Oliver Hrubiak from Matlock in Derbyshire.

T-shirt design

Simon runs the

"I really enjoyed my four months of training," says Simon, "but it wasn't the first time I'd run a marathon. I ran the London Marathon in 1998, completing it in three and half hours, and I wanted to better that time. I needed to concentrate on speed and stamina and I found myself the perfect running partner in Roger Black, one of Britain's greatest 400-metres runners. This was Roger's first marathon so, whilst I could get tips on speed, I could give Roger advice on what to expect."

Simon's preparations didn't end with the training. To record the race, he had to meet Blue Peter cameras at 10 points around the course. He also had to test an unusual camera worn by fellow-runner Nadeem Sheikh, who agreed to run as far as he could with Simon.

It was a beautiful sunny day and the whole route was lined with Blue Peter viewers who had come out to cheer Simon on. Everyone who saw him was certain that Simon would finish, he was running so strongly. The question was whether he would finish in the time he wanted.

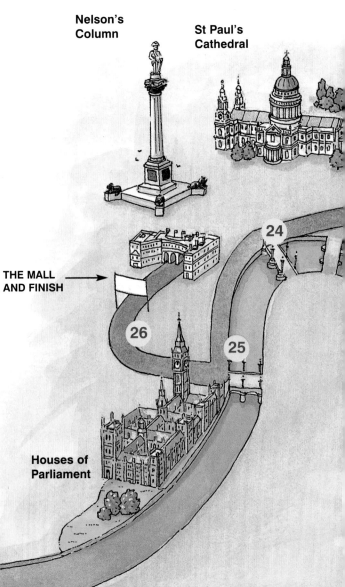

Nelson's Column

St Paul's Cathedral

THE MALL AND FINISH →

24

26

25

Houses of Parliament

At eight o'clock on the morning of the race, everyone had gathered at Blackheath in south-east London. Over 30,000 runners were ready to run 26.2 miles. Konnie and Matt were among over 1000 volunteers working with St John Ambulance who were on hand to give first-aid treatment along the route – whilst Katy waited for Simon at the half-way point, Tower Bridge.

Running the 2000 London Marathon was one of the biggest challenges given to any of the Blue Peter presenters this year. It was one that Simon took up.

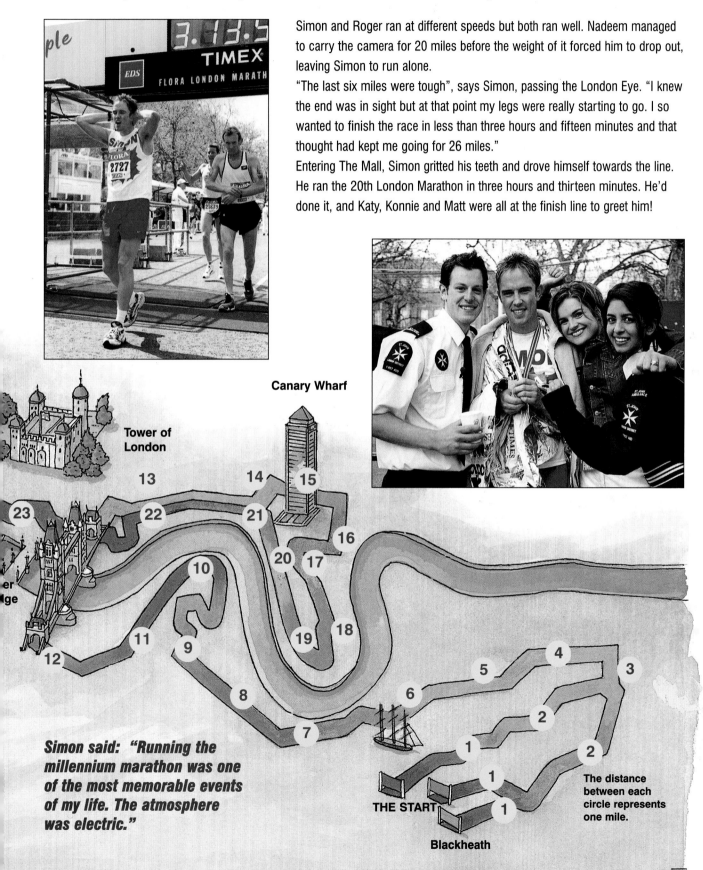

Simon and Roger ran at different speeds but both ran well. Nadeem managed to carry the camera for 20 miles before the weight of it forced him to drop out, leaving Simon to run alone.

"The last six miles were tough", says Simon, passing the London Eye. "I knew the end was in sight but at that point my legs were really starting to go. I so wanted to finish the race in less than three hours and fifteen minutes and that thought had kept me going for 26 miles."

Entering The Mall, Simon gritted his teeth and drove himself towards the line. He ran the 20th London Marathon in three hours and thirteen minutes. He'd done it, and Katy, Konnie and Matt were all at the finish line to greet him!

Canary Wharf

Tower of
London

Simon said: "Running the millennium marathon was one of the most memorable events of my life. The atmosphere was electric."

THE START

The distance
between each
circle represents
one mile.

Blackheath

Matt dressed as Corporal of Horse to tell the amazing story of Freddy the horse who served in the Boer War. Afterwards Freddy was awarded the Queen's South Africa medal – the only animal to receive one.

Well what can you say? Katy as you've never seen her before or will again!

Doesn't he look the gentleman? Simon went to Greenwich and stepped back in time to tell the story of John Harrison, who unlocked the secrets of longitude that changed the world forever.

"Mangez!" A queenly Clare Bradley on a visit to Marie Antoinette's farm at Versailles.

Looking quite at home in the Officers' Mess. Hope no one in the RAF spots him as an impostor!

Not an instantly recognisable pair. Mabel and Matt playing the parts of Mick the Miller and his movie director. Mick the Miller started his career as a greyhound racer at Wembley Stadium before becoming a movie star. Mick's finest film was 'Wild Boy' made in 1933.

It may be raining, but Katy's still the belle of the ball!

Milk, no sugar, thank you! Matt living it up in one of London's most stylish gentlemen's tailors.

Has it worked? Simon was promised the Dead Sea mud would be good for his skin.

Snappy Dressers!

Whose turn next? Simon and Konnie dressed for ten-pin bowling. An early form was played in Ancient Egypt and thousands of years later ninepins were all the rage in Holland. Dutch immigrants introduced the sport to America in the 17th century.

History comes to life with a change of clothes. Matt went underground dressed like Rob Kelly, one of the miners who lost his life in the 1897 Snaefell Mine disaster on the Isle of Man.

51

How to Draw the Blue Peter Ship

Tony Hart designed the ship back in 1963 and since then it's appeared on over a million badges. Here's the ingenious way to draw it ...

1 Gather together a selection of circular objects, such as bottle tops, a roll of tape, cups and aerosol lids. You will also need a bottle opener (like the one shown above) a ruler, a pen and a pencil.

2 Use the different objects to practise drawing the different sized arcs. Objects which have diameters of approximately 12, 10, 7, 5 and 2 centimetres will be very useful.

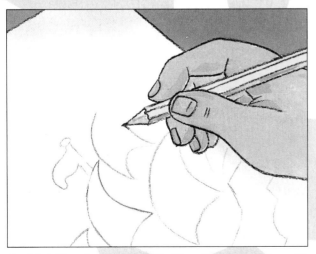

3 Lightly sketch the outline of the ship with a pencil. Don't worry about getting this exactly right, it is just a guide to help you.

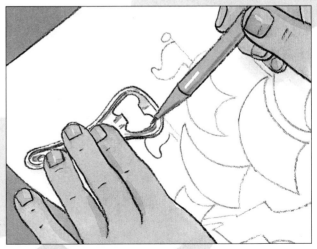

4 Use the bottle opener to draw the wiggly lines of the flag.

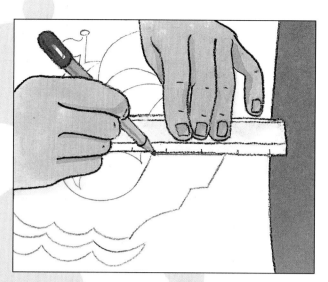

5 Now, using the circular objects you have selected, draw around part of each curved edge to form the sails. Use the largest object for the middle sail and the next largest for the other three.

6 Draw the sides of the hull and the masts, using your ruler.

7 Use the smaller objects to finish the hull and add waves, as shown.

8 Finally, colour your Blue Peter ship to make a real splash!

Whether skiing or snowboarding, Katy has always proved herself quite a star on the snow slopes. So we all wondered how she would do when she tried out three winter sports in Igls, near Innsbruck in Austria.

READY FOR ACTION – Katy gets to grips with the snowbike with Captain Sarah Bradley-Walker.

DOWNHILL

JUST TIME FOR A QUICK PHOTO with Sean, Chris and Eric before Katy's thrilling descent down the track.

KATY WAS AMAZED by the amount of polishing and preparation that goes into the sleigh. Before each run, the team makes sure that it's as slick and as smooth as possible, all to get the best time. *Below:* Serious courage – Katy holds on tight as she attempts the Skeleton run.

ALL THE WAY!

Katy's first challenge was the snowbike, which is simply a bicycle frame and 4 skis, 2 of which are attached to the bike, with the others worn by the rider for balance. Sitting far back on the saddle, and keeping her arms straight with her hands on the handlebars, Katy set off. It was very bouncy going down the slopes and lots of fun!

Next up was the bobsleigh, which can zoom down the track at speeds of around 100 miles an hour. She met up with the British four-man bobsleigh team who were busy training for the next Winter Olympics. Sergeant Sean Olsson told Katy that during the run it was important she kept her helmet away from the person in front otherwise she might push their head forwards and stop them from seeing where they're going. 'What if it turns over?' asked Katy. 'Don't panic, keep your head down and hang on!' 14 000 metres and 14 corners later, it was all over and Katy's grin said it all!

Katy thought nothing could be scarier than the bobsleigh but that was before she attempted the Skeleton. You need to have serious courage to speed down an icy track headfirst on a metal tray. After a lot of practice, Katy was ready to attempt this terrifying run. She was given a push off. There was no turning back – she hung on very tight as she hurtled down the track, hitting the walls and trying to remember everything she'd been taught – keep your head down, point your toes and steer with your shoulders. Halfway down, Katy couldn't see a thing because her helmet had steamed up. It was faster than she'd imagined and finished far too quickly. And her verdict? "That was cool and I'm all in one piece!"

Stargazing

Look up at the sky on a clear night and what do you see? Thousands of stars perhaps, but can you find your way around the night sky? Blue Peter astronomer Anton Vamplew is our guide to the stars and planets and here are his suggested four places to start stargazing.

Great Globular in Hercules

The constellation of Hercules is visible from spring to mid-autumn, together with its famous globular cluster. It is only just visible to the unaided eye, so try to borrow a pair of binoculars. Radio broadcasts have been speeding towards this cluster since 16 November 1974, when we sent our first and only intentional message to anyone, or anything, that might be listening in space. So far, the message has only travelled one-thousandth of the distance of 25,000 light-years. And even if there is anything there to receive it and transmit a reply, it will be the year AD 51974 before it reaches Earth.

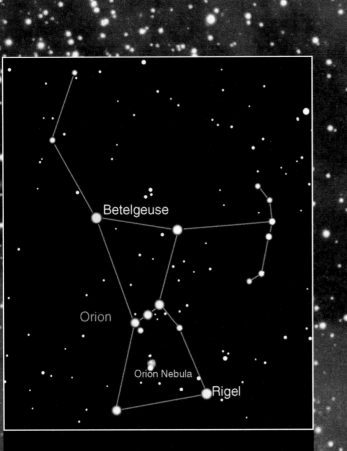

Orion and the Orion Nebula

Over winter and early spring Orion the Hunter is visible, the brightest constellation in the whole night sky. You'll find him on the opposite side of the sky to the North Star. Orion contains stars with some great names and great colours, including the red supergiant Betelgeuse (sometimes pronounced Beetle-Juice), and the blue giant Rigel. Below Orion's Belt is a faint fuzzy patch. It's a vast cloud of gas known as the Orion Nebula, where over 500 stars are being born right now! If you can borrow a pair of binoculars it is well worth taking a look.

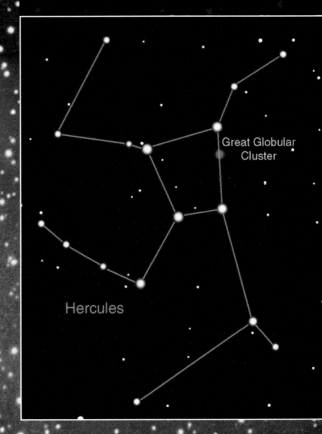

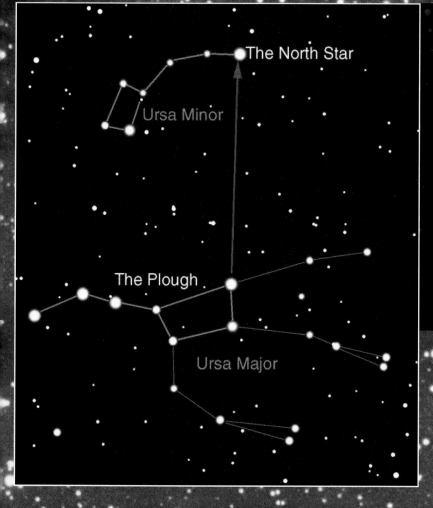

The North Star

Ursa Minor

The Plough

Ursa Major

The Plough and the North Star

The night sky can seem confusing when you're new to stargazing, but it can become an easy map to read. The best place to start is a well-known group of stars known as the Plough, part of the constellation Ursa Major, the Great Bear. The Plough looks like a saucepan with its handle outstretched to the left. It's a useful landmark and can be used to find many things in the night sky – the most famous being the North Star. Simply follow the two furthest right stars of the Plough upwards and you will reach this shining point of light. It's only the 48th brightest star in the sky – not THE brightest, as myth has it. In fact, if you see a very brilliant point of light, it's more likely to be a planet than a star!

The Andromeda Galaxy

From late summer to the end of winter you have a chance to see the furthest thing visible to the unaided eye, the Andromeda Galaxy. You can only see it clearly from areas where the sky is really dark, away from the light pollution of towns and cities. It's a nearby galaxy, slightly larger than our own, containing perhaps 300,000 million stars, and it appears as a faint, smudgy patch. It's 20 quintillion kilometres away (that's 20 followed by 18 zeros) and light from it takes over 2 million years to reach us!

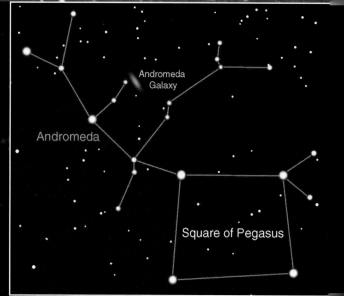

Andromeda
Galaxy

Andromeda

Square of Pegasus

Happy Stargazing

Blue Peter
Out and About

AND GETTING IN FREE!

THE BLUE PETER TEAM is always travelling around the UK checking out new exhibitions and places of special interest. If we think they will be enjoyed by viewers, we always have an extra question, 'can Blue Peter badge winners get in free?' Luckily, most are pleased to say yes and they get added to our ever-growing list of places that won't charge an entrance fee if you are under 16 and wearing a Blue Peter badge.

If you are out and about with your family and are looking for somewhere to spend the day, here are a few places that get the Blue Peter thumbs-up.

Always phone and check opening times before making a special trip.

Stratford-upon-Avon is one of the most popular tourist destinations in England because it's in Shakespeare country. Step back in time and visit the very house where Shakespeare, the world's most famous playwright, was born in 1564. It has been beautifully renovated so that it looks exactly as it would have done when Shakespeare was a boy. Take a stroll in the garden which is filled with the same varieties of plants that would have grown there nearly 500 years ago. A Blue Peter competition winner designed a flag to celebrate the reopening of his birthplace – you might see it flying outside.

Longleat House and Safari Park in Warminster, Wiltshire, is famous for its lions and magnificent setting. The house is one of the finest examples of Elizabethan architecture in Britain and is filled with historic treasures and heirlooms. In the grounds, you'll find the world's longest hedge maze, as well as lions, tigers, monkeys and giraffe roaming the Safari Park.

World of Glass is a brand new exhibition at St Helens in Merseyside. You can visit its tunnels, hear the story of glass and learn how it's made. There are fascinating glass-blowing exhibitions and a magic mirror maze to see who is the 'fairest of them all!'

Carrickfergus in Co. Antrim boasts one of the finest Norman castles in Ireland. You can explore medieval life here and meet a host of characters like Adam the Archer, Simon the Sentry and Godfrey the Gatekeeper who tell the turbulent history of the castle. It's also a beautiful place to enjoy a picnic lunch.

CAT is a unique visitor centre, located in the Snowdonia National Park at Machynlleth in Powys. CAT stands for Centre for Alternative Technology and has an exciting range of interactive displays including wind, water and solar power. Visitors enter the centre by water-powered cliff railway. If you want to know more about sustainable technologies and lifestyles, this eco-centre is an eye-opening place.

CHOCOLATE BROWNIES

Chocolate brownies are a must for any party. To make 12 to 16 delectable chocolate squares follow this easy recipe and your friends and family will be amazed at your culinary skills.

INGREDIENTS

100g butter
225g golden caster sugar
40g cocoa powder
2 eggs
1 teaspoon vanilla essence
50g self-raising flour
50g chocolate chips

METHOD

Put the butter in a small pan and melt over a low heat. Take the pan off the heat and stir in the cocoa powder, making sure you remove any lumps.

Beat the eggs in a large bowl. Add the sugar and mix until smooth. Now put the cocoa mixture into the egg mixture and stir thoroughly before adding vanilla essence. Gradually add the self-raising flour through a sieve and keep stirring until it becomes a sticky mixture. Finally, add the chocolate chips.

Line a shallow square or oblong cake tin with greaseproof paper. Transfer the mixture to the tin and place in the middle of a preheated oven at 180°C or gas mark 4 for around 30 minutes. The chocolate brownies will be crispy on top and gooey in the middle. Leave them in the tin for roughly 10 minutes before cutting into squares. Carefully transfer them to a cooling rack and wait until they are cool enough to eat.

Now simply enjoy!

You could win a day at the
Blue Peter studio!

The winner, with friend and family (maximum 4 persons), will be able to spend a day with members of the Blue Peter team in the studio. The winner's transport costs to the studio will be provided.

Simply answer this question and you're in with a chance. Good luck!

What country did the Blue Peter team visit during the summer of 2000?

- Competition entries must be received by 26 January 2001.
- Venue and visit date will be agreed with the winner.
- The winner will be notified by post no later than 1 March 2001.
- Send your answer, along with your name, age and address to: **Blue Peter Competition, Egmont World Limited, Deanway Technology Centre, Wilmslow Road, Handforth, Cheshire SK9 3FB.**
- *REMEMBER! COMPETITION CLOSING DATE IS 26 JANUARY 2001.*

RULES

1 Entrants must be under 16 years of age.
2 One winner will be chosen at random and notified by post.
3 The judges' decision will be final. No correspondence can be entered into.
4 A list of winners will be made available on request from Egmont World Limited, Deanway Technology Centre, Wilmslow Road, Handforth, Cheshire SK9 3FB after 26 January 2001. Please enclose a s.a.e.
5 Employees (and their relatives) of Egmont World Limited and their associated companies are not eligible to enter.
6 Entries are limited to one per person.
7 The competition is open to residents of the UK, Ireland and the Channel Islands.
8 The publishers reserve the right to vary the prizes, subject to availability.

Our address is: Blue Peter, BBC TV,London W12 7RJ
Our home page is: www.bbc.co.uk/bluepeter
e-mail: bluepeter@bbc.co.uk

ACKNOWLEDGEMENTS

Artworks
Simon Girling Associates: Paul Wilks, pp 42–43, Brian Hoskin, pp 48–49
Garden Chimes: Margaret Parnell, pp 30–31,
Cardigan Cushions: Gillian Shearing, pp 20–21

PHOTOGRAPHIC ACKNOWLEDGEMENTS
Chris Capstick, pp 30–31, 16–17, 40, 28–29 Galaxy Picture Library: Michael Stecker,
pp 56–57 Martyn Goddard, pp 2–3, 4–5, 20–21, 41, 60–61, 62–63 Zena Holloway,
p19 Sharkey, pp 26–27 Jonathan Reeves, pp 36–37 Felicia Webb, pp 32–33 Telegraph
Picture Library, pp 32–33 Chris Cole, pp 48–49 Edinburgh & Lothians Tourist Board,
pp 34–35 The Shakespeare Birthplace Trust, p58, Stuart Rayner, p59

All other photographs are © Blue Peter and were taken by Richard Marson, Alex Leger,
Bridget Caldwell, Joanna Robinson and lots of Blue Peter viewers. If we have left
anyone out we're sorry.
The authors would like to specially thank Clare Eades, Cassie Harman and the whole of
the Blue Peter team for their help and ideas.

Every effort has been made to contact the copyright holders for permission to reproduce
material in this book. If any material has been included without permission please
contact the publisher.